TWO AND A HALF ACRES OF FAITH
STUDY GUIDE

Copyright © 2025 by Jay S. Miller

Published by Four Rivers Media

All rights reserved. No portion of this book may be reproduced, stored in a retrieval system, or transmitted in any form or by any means—electronic, mechanical, photocopy, recording, scanning, or other—except for brief quotations in critical reviews or articles, without prior written permission of the author.

Unless otherwise specified, all Scripture quotations are taken from the Holy Bible, New International Version®, NIV®. Copyright © 1973, 1978, 1984, 2011 by Biblica, Inc.™ Used by permission of Zondervan. All rights reserved worldwide. www.zondervan.com. The "NIV" and "New International Version" are trademarks registered in the United States Patent and Trademark Office by Biblica, Inc.™ | Scripture quotations marked ESV are from The ESV® Bible (The Holy Bible, English Standard Version®), copyright © 2001 by Crossway, a publishing ministry of Good News Publishers. Used by permission. |All rights reserved. | Scripture quotations marked NKJV are taken from the New King James Version®. Copyright © 1982 by Thomas Nelson. Used by permission. All rights reserved.

For foreign and subsidiary rights, contact the author.

Cover design by Sara Young
Cover photo by Jansen Miller

ISBN: 978-1-964794-28-0   1 2 3 4 5 6 7 8 9 10

Printed in the United States of America

TWO AND A HALF ACRES OF FAITH

How Faith Builds When Dreams Crumble

JAY S. MILLER

STUDY GUIDE

FOUR

CONTENTS

CHAPTER 1. **JUST ONE WORD** 6

CHAPTER 2. **JUST SIXTY DOLLARS AND A DREAM** 10

CHAPTER 3. **ALL I WANT IS A FAMILY** 14

CHAPTER 4. **THE DREAM IS DEAD** 18

CHAPTER 5. **ONE STEP AT A TIME** 22

CHAPTER 6. **MOM, LOOK, I CAN WALK AGAIN!** 26

CHAPTER 7. **FINALLY, A FAMILY!** 30

CHAPTER 8. **YOU HAVE THIRTY DAYS** 34

CHAPTER 9. **NO ONE BUT JESUS** 38

CHAPTER 10. **WORK YOUR DREAM** 42

CHAPTER 11. **MY TWO MIRACLE BABIES** 46

CHAPTER 12. **IF MY MOM DIES** 50

CHAPTER 13. **WHAT WILL YOU PASS DOWN?** 56

CHAPTER 14. **WHEN PRAYERS DON'T WORK** 60

CHAPTER 15. **I'M IN HAWAII** 66

CHAPTER 16. **HAPPY MOTHER'S DAY, JEAN!** 72

CHAPTER 17. **WE BUILT A FAMILY** 76

TWO AND A HALF ACRES OF FAITH

How Faith Builds When Dreams Crumble

JAY S. MILLER

CHAPTER 1

JUST ONE WORD

Just one word from God can change everything.

READING TIME

As you read Chapter 1: "Just One Word" in *Two and a Half Acres of Faith*, review, reflect on, and respond to the text by answering the following questions.

REVIEW, REFLECT, AND RESPOND

Have you ever felt a strong nudge or calling in your life? How did you respond to it, and what was the outcome?

_____
_____
_____
_____
_____
_____
_____
_____
_____
_____

What is a promise or word from God you hold onto, and how has it shaped your journey?

_____
_____
_____
_____
_____
_____
_____
_____
_____
_____

> *"When My word goes forth, it will not return to Me empty; it will accomplish what I desire and achieve the purpose for which I sent it."*
>
> —Isaiah 55:11 (author paraphrase)

Consider the scripture above and answer the following questions:

How does Isaiah 55:11 challenge you to trust that God's plans will succeed, even when obstacles seem insurmountable? Have you ever seen this come to pass in your own life? Describe your experience.

_____

_____

_____

_____

_____

_____

How could you apply this scripture practically to your life?

_____

_____

_____

_____

_____

_____

Have you ever faced a situation where faith seemed illogical but necessary? How did it end?

_____

_____

_____

If God called you to take a step of faith today that seemed beyond your resources or abilities, what would your response be, and why?

What is a dream or goal in your life where you need to trust God more deeply for guidance?

Are you in need of a word from God? How can you start seeking God's guidance with all your heart?

CHAPTER 2

JUST SIXTY DOLLARS AND A DREAM

*Don't you dare discount yourself
before the journey even starts.*

READING TIME

As you read Chapter 2: "Just Sixty Dollars and a Dream" in Two and a Half Acres of Faith, *review, reflect on, and respond to the text by answering the following questions.*

REVIEW, REFLECT, AND RESPOND

Reflect on a time when you questioned if God was speaking to you. How did you handle that uncertainty, and what did you learn about how to discern between God's voice and your own?

_____
_____
_____
_____
_____
_____
_____
_____
_____

Why do you think God calls His people to a dream when the odds of its fulfillment are stacked against them?

_____
_____
_____
_____
_____
_____
_____
_____
_____

> *"My sheep hear my voice, and I know them, and they follow me."*
>
> —John 10:27 (ESV)

Consider the scripture above and answer the following questions:

How does this scripture aid in your efforts to distinguish between your voice and God's voice? In what ways does it instill confidence that you are being led by the Holy Spirit?

_____
_____
_____
_____

How does this scripture illustrate the relationship between Jesus and His followers when facing daunting challenges that demand significant steps of faith?

_____
_____
_____
_____

Reflect on a time when you pursued a dream that others doubted. How did their doubts affect your confidence, and how did you rely on God to persevere?

_____
_____
_____
_____

Imagine you were driving toward God's promise with just sixty dollars and a dream. What thoughts or emotions would you be battling? Have you ever been in a similar position, and how did it unfold?

Think about a time when hesitation held you back in the face of the unknown. How would taking action have changed the outcome?

What has been the loudest voice in your life recently—faith or fear? How can you amplify the voice of faith in times of uncertainty?

CHAPTER 3

ALL I WANT IS A FAMILY

Like a flower pushing through the cracks in the hardest ground, hope begins to grow in places we least expect.

READING TIME

As you read Chapter 3: "All I Want Is a Family" in *Two and a Half Acres of Faith*, review, reflect on, and respond to the text by answering the following questions.

REVIEW, REFLECT, AND RESPOND

Reflect on a dream you've had that has been delayed or shattered. How have you processed that disappointment, and what has it revealed about your faith?

_____
_____
_____
_____
_____
_____
_____
_____
_____

How has a personal loss or failure challenged your understanding of God's goodness and faithfulness?

_____
_____
_____
_____
_____
_____
_____
_____
_____

> *"For I know the plans I have for you," declares the LORD, "plans to prosper you and not to harm you, plans to give you hope and a future."*
>
> —Jeremiah 29:11

Consider the scripture above and answer the following questions:

This scripture promises that God's plans are always good, but they weren't visible for Jean and Sterling in their pain. Looking back on a difficult time in your life, where can you now see evidence of God working for your good?

_____
_____
_____
_____
_____

This scripture emphasizes a future filled with hope. What are you holding onto today that prevents you from fully trusting God to lead you toward the future He has planned?

_____
_____
_____
_____
_____

How do you respond when something you desire deeply feels like it will never come to pass?

_____
_____
_____

When you've faced repeated setbacks, what has kept you going—or tempted you to give up entirely?

Think back to a time when God's timing proved to be perfect. How might the outcome have been different if what you were waiting for had happened earlier, according to your own timing?

How does the knowledge that your story is still unfolding encourage you to trust God with your unfinished chapters?

CHAPTER 4

THE DREAM IS DEAD

The trials you face today are shaping the testimony you will carry tomorrow.

READING TIME

As you read Chapter 4: "The Dream Is Dead" in *Two and a Half Acres of Faith*, review, reflect on, and respond to the text by answering the following questions.

REVIEW, REFLECT, AND RESPOND

Has anyone ever told you to give up on something important to you? How did their words affect your faith and determination?

_____
_____
_____
_____
_____
_____
_____
_____
_____

unrelenting pain, what emotions or thoughts challenge your ability to trust God? Do you let bitterness take root?

_____
_____
_____
_____
_____
_____
_____
_____
_____
_____

> *"And we know that in all things God works for the good of those who love Him, who have been called according to His purpose."*
>
> —Romans 8:28

Consider the scripture above and answer the following questions:

How does this scripture highlight the difference between experiencing only good things and having all things—both good and bad—transformed for good? Why is the latter ultimately more impactful and meaningful?

_____
_____
_____
_____
_____

Think about a situation in your life that seemed hopeless at the time but later revealed God's purpose. How does that experience shape your ability to trust Him in current uncertainties?

_____
_____
_____
_____
_____

Think about a dream or desire you've buried. How might God be preparing it for a future "blooming" season?

_____
_____
_____

What emotional wounds have lingered in your life, and where do you see God's hand in your healing process?

In what areas do you sense God refining you, and how do you envision that refinement playing a role in healing wounds or molding your faith?

Is there an area of your life where you feel compelled to move too quickly? What fears or insecurities might be driving that urgency?

CHAPTER 5

ONE STEP AT A TIME

It's not about how big your faith is; it's about the One in whom your faith rests.

READING TIME

As you read Chapter 5: "One Step at a Time" in *Two and a Half Acres of Faith*, review, reflect on, and respond to the text by answering the following questions.

REVIEW, REFLECT, AND RESPOND

What "steps" in your life represent faith in action to claim God's promise, even if the outcome isn't clear?

_____
_____
_____
_____
_____
_____
_____
_____

This chapter emphasizes the power of small beginnings. Reflect on a time when you underestimated the value of a small act of faith. How did it lead to something greater than you expected?

_____
_____
_____
_____
_____
_____
_____
_____
_____
_____

> *"If you have faith as small as a mustard seed, you can say to this mountain, 'Move from here to there,' and it will move. Nothing will be impossible for you."*
>
> —Matthew 17:20

Consider the scripture above and answer the following questions:

This verse illustrates the power of even small faith. When have you felt that your faith wasn't enough, and how does this scripture challenge that belief?

_____
_____
_____
_____
_____

How does the imagery of a mustard seed help you reframe your expectations about what God can do with the small steps you've already taken?

_____
_____
_____
_____
_____

How does this demonstrate that a seemingly closed door doesn't mean you should stop pursuing, especially if God has been directing your steps all along?

_____
_____
_____

What situations in your life require you to look past the present reality and see the bigger picture of what could be?

When has acting on faith required you to do something uncomfortable or unconventional? How did it shape your relationship with God?

The two-and-a-half acres represented more than land; it was a promise coming to life. What promises or dreams in your life feel like they are still waiting to be fulfilled, and how are you actively preparing for them?

CHAPTER 6

MOM, LOOK, I CAN WALK AGAIN!

What do you have in your hand? And more importantly, are you willing to give it to God?

READING TIME

As you read Chapter 6: "Mom, Look, I Can Walk Again!" in *Two and a Half Acres of Faith*, review, reflect on, and respond to the text by answering the following questions.

REVIEW, REFLECT, AND RESPOND

When have you experienced a battle between fear and faith? Which one prevailed, and what influenced the outcome?

_____
_____
_____
_____
_____
_____
_____
_____

Has there been a moment in your life when you witnessed or experienced something that you could only attribute to God? How did it impact your belief in Him?

_____
_____
_____
_____
_____
_____
_____
_____

In what areas of life might you be waiting for God to act, though He is waiting for you to take a step of faith?

_____
_____
_____
_____
_____
_____
_____
_____
_____
_____

How do you actively engage with your faith rather than wait passively for answers?

_____
_____
_____
_____
_____
_____
_____
_____
_____
_____
_____

The chapter underscores the tension of witnessing suffering while believing in God's goodness. When have you struggled to reconcile God's goodness with the pain you or someone close to you experienced? How do you view that experience now, looking back?

_____
_____
_____
_____
_____
_____
_____
_____
_____

Think about a moment in your life that could serve as a testimony to others. How do you share that story in a way that honors God?

_____
_____
_____
_____
_____
_____
_____
_____
_____

CHAPTER 7

FINALLY, A FAMILY!

> *In the moments when life feels chaotic or beyond your control, He is still sovereign, still present, and still faithful.*

READING TIME

As you read Chapter 7: "Finally, a Family!" in *Two and a Half Acres of Faith*, review, reflect on, and respond to the text by answering the following questions.

REVIEW, REFLECT, AND RESPOND

Reflect on a time when a long-awaited promise was fulfilled in your life. What emotions did you feel, and how did that moment reshape your faith?

_____
_____
_____
_____
_____
_____
_____
_____
_____

What blessings in your life do you now cherish more deeply because of the struggles it took to receive them?

_____
_____
_____
_____
_____
_____
_____
_____
_____

> *"Come to me, all you who are weary and burdened, and I will give you rest."*
>
> —Matthew 11:28

Consider the scripture above and answer the following questions:

In your own words, what is biblical rest? How do you know when you've entered into a state of rest amid a particularly challenging circumstance?

_____
_____
_____
_____
_____

Jesus invites the weary and burdened to come to Him. What burdens are you holding onto that you find difficult to surrender, and what fears or hesitations keep you from fully accepting His rest?

_____
_____
_____
_____
_____

What has been a defining moment in your life that confirmed God's faithfulness to you? How did it change the way you see Him?

_____
_____
_____
_____

This chapter illustrates the profound joy of receiving after enduring. What role does gratitude play in your life after you've received something you've prayed for? How do you continue to honor God in that joy?

Have you ever received something from God, only to have it ripped out of your hands? How did you respond to that, and what do you believe about it now?

In what ways could God's work in preparing you for something greater be disguised as moments where you are slipping away or moving further away from the promise?

CHAPTER 8

YOU HAVE THIRTY DAYS

His arms are wide open, ready to catch every fragment of your pain and turn it into something beautiful.

READING TIME

As you read Chapter 8: "You Have Thirty Days" in *Two and a Half Acres of Faith*, review, reflect on, and respond to the text by answering the following questions.

REVIEW, REFLECT, AND RESPOND

What has been the most difficult act of surrender you've faced, and how did you trust God through it?

_____
_____
_____
_____
_____
_____
_____
_____
_____

When have you had to continue showing love and care in a situation where letting go was inevitable?

_____
_____
_____
_____
_____
_____
_____
_____
_____

> *"He heals the brokenhearted and binds up their wounds."*
>
> —Psalm 147:3

Consider the scripture above and answer the following questions:

Healing often takes time and requires trust. How do you respond when God's process of binding your wounds feels slower than you hoped or expected?

___

This verse emphasizes God's care for the brokenhearted. What wounds do you still carry? How has God cared for you through them?

___

When have you had to take bold action with no certainty of the outcome? What was the result, and how did it grow your faith?

___

What do you think is behind the myth that the presence of fear is always a signal to give up and walk away?

The journey through immense loss and unavailable resources often requires vulnerability and asking others for help. When have you had to set aside pride and lean on others in faith?

The chapter illustrates that faith often grows under pressure. Reflect on a season when you felt stretched or tested. How did that time deepen your intimacy with God?

CHAPTER 9

NO ONE BUT JESUS

Though the path ahead may be unclear, know that God is already there, preparing the way.

READING TIME

As you read Chapter 9: "No One but Jesus" in Two and a Half Acres of Faith, review, reflect on, and respond to the text by answering the following questions.

REVIEW, REFLECT, AND RESPOND

Have you ever experienced a moment where everything else in your life seemed to fail, leaving you with no one but Jesus? What story did He write for you during that time, and how does it fit into your story now?

_____
_____
_____
_____
_____
_____
_____
_____

The chapter emphasizes surrendering completely to Jesus. Reflect on an area of your life where you've resisted surrender. What fears or doubts have kept you from fully trusting Him with that part of your life?

_____
_____
_____
_____
_____
_____
_____
_____

> *"Faith is the assurance of things hoped for, the conviction of things not seen."*
>
> —Hebrews 11:1 (ESV)

Consider the scripture above and answer the following questions:

This verse challenges us to have assurance in God's character, not our circumstances. What truths about God's character can shift your perspective away from your current circumstances?

_____
_____
_____
_____
_____

Faith requires hope for what is unseen. Are there areas in your life where you find it difficult to hold onto hope? What makes it harder to find hope in that area and easier in others? How does God's Word challenge the notion that hope is situation-specific?

_____
_____
_____
_____
_____

Reflect on a moment when you doubted God's presence in your suffering. What eventually helped you see or believe that He was with you all along?

_____
_____
_____

When have you sought comfort, answers, or healing in something or someone other than Jesus? How did that pursuit affect you, and what brought you back to Him?

What difficulties have you encountered during seasons where Jesus was your only source of support? Reflect on moments when glimpses of hope broke through—how did they help ease the weight of your desperation?

The chapter concludes with the reminder that Jesus is always enough. What does it mean to you personally that Jesus is sufficient for every need, even when life feels overwhelming or incomplete?

CHAPTER 10

WORK YOUR DREAM

While prayer is the bedrock of every dream, faith without action is like a fire without fuel.

READING TIME

As you read Chapter 10: "Work Your Dream" in Two and a Half Acres of Faith, *review, reflect on, and respond to the text by answering the following questions.*

REVIEW, REFLECT, AND RESPOND

What does putting in effort look like in your current circumstances, and what steps have you already taken toward it?

_____
_____
_____
_____
_____
_____
_____
_____
_____

How do practical action steps demonstrate your belief in His promises? How does this apply to your current season?

_____
_____
_____
_____
_____
_____
_____
_____
_____

> *"Whatever your hand finds to do,
> do it with all your might."*
>
> —Ecclesiastes 9:10

Consider the scripture above and answer the following questions:

This verse emphasizes giving your full effort to the work at hand. Reflect on something you are currently pursuing—are you truly giving it your all, or are distractions, fear, or complacency holding you back?

_____

_____

_____

_____

_____

Consider the ways you spend your energy and focus. Are there areas of your life where you are exerting effort on things that don't align with your God-given purpose? How can you redirect that effort?

_____

_____

_____

_____

_____

The chapter describes how working the dream required sacrifices and perseverance. Reflect on a time when pursuing a dream required you to give up comfort, time, or security. How did these sacrifices give birth to the dream?

_____

_____

_____

_____

_____

Dreams don't just happen; they require intentional effort. When have you mistakenly expected progress to come without work? How did that realization change the way you approached your goals?

_____

_____

_____

_____

Reflect on a time when you faced a major setback while pursuing something important. How did you recover, and what did you learn about yourself in the process?

_____

_____

_____

_____

The chapter highlights the value of consistent, faithful effort. What has been the hardest part of staying consistent in your faith or working toward a goal? How has God met you in those moments of struggle?

_____

_____

_____

_____

CHAPTER 11

MY TWO MIRACLE BABIES

Those dreams, the ones that stir deep within your soul, are not there by accident.

READING TIME

As you read Chapter 11: "My Two Miracle Babies" in *Two and a Half Acres of Faith*, review, reflect on, and respond to the text by answering the following questions.

REVIEW, REFLECT, AND RESPOND

Is there a promise or prayer you are still waiting to see fulfilled? How does reflecting on past miracles help you trust Him for the future?

_____
_____
_____
_____
_____
_____
_____
_____
_____

When have you experienced a season of joy that followed deep sorrow? How did it change your understanding of God's ability to redeem difficult situations?

_____
_____
_____
_____
_____
_____
_____
_____
_____

> *"Now to Him who is able to do exceedingly abundantly above all that we ask or think, according to the power that works in us."*
>
> —Ephesians 3:20 (NKJV)

Consider the scripture above and answer the following questions:

Reflect on a time when God exceeded your expectations in a way you didn't anticipate. What comes up for you when you consider how God's dream for you might be much bigger than the one in your heart right now?

_____
_____
_____
_____
_____

This scripture points to God's plans being far greater than our own. Reflect on a time when your plans fell apart, but God's greater purpose prevailed. How did that experience reshape your trust in Him?

_____
_____
_____
_____
_____

The chapter highlights the joy of receiving a blessing after years of loss. What blessing in your life feels especially meaningful because of the challenges it took to receive it?

_____
_____

When have you felt like giving up but found a renewed sense of hope that carried you through? What sparked that hope?

Reflect on a time when God fulfilled a desire of your heart in a way you didn't anticipate. How did His plan differ from your own, and what did you learn from it?

What is one dream or goal in your life that you are actively working toward with faith, and what would it mean to see it fulfilled?

CHAPTER 12

IF MY MOM DIES

The trials you face today are temporary, but the work God is doing in and through you has eternal significance.

READING TIME

As you read Chapter 12: "If My Mom Dies" in *Two and a Half Acres of Faith*, review, reflect on, and respond to the text by answering the following questions.

REVIEW, REFLECT, AND RESPOND

This chapter highlights biblical figures like Noah, Abraham, Paul, and Joseph, who remained faithful to God despite overwhelming trials. Which of their stories resonates most with your own experience, and how does their example challenge you to persist in serving God, no matter what is taken from you?

_____
_____
_____
_____
_____
_____
_____
_____
_____
_____

The idea of God being in control can feel abstract during times of deep pain and confusion. Reflect on what it means to truly believe that God is in control, even when life feels chaotic. How do you reconcile this truth with your own moments of anger or doubt?

_____
_____
_____

> "Trust in the LORD with all your heart and lean not on your own understanding; in all your ways submit to Him, and He will make your paths straight."
>
> —Proverbs 3:5-6

Consider the scripture above and answer the following questions:

This scripture promises that God will make your paths straight. When have you experienced God redirecting your path after you submitted to Him? What was the ebb and flow of that experience like?

The phrase "lean not on your own understanding" suggests a deliberate choice to trust God over what seems logical or comfortable. When have you chosen to rely on your own understanding to make sense of a situation, and how did it impact your experience as you waited for God's plan to unfold?

_____
_____
_____
_____
_____
_____
_____
_____
_____

Noah spent decades building an ark while facing ridicule, trusting God's word despite no visible evidence. Reflect on a time when you felt called to obey God in a way that seemed foolish or unnecessary. Did you stay faithful? Why or why not?

_____
_____
_____
_____
_____
_____
_____
_____
_____

Have you ever felt angry at God? How did that anger impact your relationship with Him, and what steps did you take (or need to take) to work through it?

_____
_____
_____
_____
_____
_____
_____
_____
_____
_____
_____

How does it feel to know that God is in control? Does it provide comfort? Anxiety? Uncertainty? Explain.

_____
_____
_____
_____
_____
_____

What does it mean to "fight the good fight of faith" in the midst of loss and disappointment?

CHAPTER 13

WHAT WILL YOU PASS DOWN?

Faith is a legacy that transcends time, and it's our responsibility to steward that gift well.

READING TIME

As you read Chapter 13: "What Will You Pass Down?" in *Two and a Half Acres of Faith*, review, reflect on, and respond to the text by answering the following questions.

REVIEW, REFLECT, AND RESPOND

If your life ended today, what would others remember most about you?

_____
_____
_____
_____
_____
_____
_____
_____
_____

What legacy do you want to leave behind for those closest to you? How do your current actions affirm or contradict that vision?

_____
_____
_____
_____
_____
_____
_____
_____
_____

> *"For all the promises of God in Him are Yes, and in Him Amen, to the glory of God through us."*
>
> —2 Corinthians 1:20 (NKJV)

Consider the scripture above and answer the following questions:

What specific promises found in God's Word has He fulfilled in your life? Why do you think we often continue to doubt, despite the overwhelming evidence that He'll do it again?

_____
_____
_____
_____
_____

Do you actively embrace and affirm God's promises with a heartfelt "Amen," or do they often remain as words you read without fully claiming them for your life?

_____
_____
_____
_____
_____

How have your responses to challenges modeled faith, strength, or doubt for those watching you?

_____
_____
_____
_____

Reflect on the spiritual heritage you've received from your family or mentors. How has it shaped your relationship with God, and what aspects of it do you want to pass down or change?

Reflect on a recent decision you made. Did it align with the kind of legacy you want to leave, or did it serve more immediate desires?

The chapter contrasts temporary success with eternal impact. Reflect on something you're working toward right now. Does it contribute to a legacy of eternal value, or is it focused more on immediate rewards?

CHAPTER 14

WHEN PRAYERS DON'T WORK

God hears every word. Even when heaven seems quiet, God is not absent.

READING TIME

As you read Chapter 14: "When Prayers Don't Work" in *Two and a Half Acres of Faith*, review, reflect on, and respond to the text by answering the following questions.

REVIEW, REFLECT, AND RESPOND

Reflect on a time when you felt like your prayers were met with silence. What do you believe God's silence might be accomplishing or teaching in your life?

_____
_____
_____
_____
_____
_____
_____
_____
_____

The chapter explores the pain of unmet expectations in prayer. Have you ever prayed for something deeply and felt disappointed by the outcome?

_____
_____
_____
_____
_____
_____
_____
_____
_____

> *"For my thoughts are not your thoughts, neither are your ways my ways," declares the LORD. "As the heavens are higher than the earth, so are my ways higher than your ways and my thoughts than your thoughts."*
>
> —Isaiah 55:8-9

Consider the scripture above and answer the following questions:

When have you struggled to accept that God's ways are different from yours? Can you think of a time when you did things your way instead of waiting on God's direction? What was the outcome?

_____
_____
_____
_____
_____
_____
_____
_____
_____
_____
_____
_____

This scripture challenges us to trust that God sees what we cannot. Reflect on a situation where hindsight revealed how God's plan was better than your own. How does that experience encourage you in your current struggles?

_____
_____

Have you ever felt like unanswered prayers were a reflection of your own shortcomings?

This chapter confronts the idea that prayer guarantees the outcome we want. How do you navigate the tension between praying with faith and trusting God with the results?

What do you think God is doing in your life right now? Is it causing discomfort? Joy? Describe your experience.

This chapter challenges us to redefine what it means for prayer to "work." What does effective prayer mean to you, and how does that perspective align with the chapter's portrayal of the true purpose and power of prayer?

CHAPTER 15

I'M IN HAWAII

Living your faith out loud isn't about being perfect or having all the answers.

READING TIME

As you read Chapter 15: "I'minHawaii" in *Two and a Half Acres of Faith*, review, reflect on, and respond to the text by answering the following questions.

REVIEW, REFLECT, AND RESPOND

This chapter highlights that we can influence others for Christ, no matter our situation. Reflect on a time when you encouraged or inspired someone despite facing your own challenges. How did that experience change the way you viewed your difficult circumstances?

_____
_____
_____
_____
_____
_____
_____
_____

Who in your life right now could benefit from hearing or seeing your faith in action, and what's stopping you from reaching out?

_____
_____
_____
_____
_____
_____
_____
_____

> *"You are the light of the world. A city set on a hill cannot be hidden."*
>
> —Matthew 5:14 (ESV)

Consider the scripture above and answer the following questions:

This passage calls you to be a visible light for Christ in the world. In what areas of your life are you tempted to "hide your light" because of fear, doubt, or discomfort?

_____

_____

_____

_____

_____

_____

_____

Being a light often means standing out in a world that values conformity. When have you felt the tension between living as a light for Christ and blending into the crowd? How did you handle it, and what did you learn?

_____

_____

_____

_____

_____

_____

_____

Have you ever questioned the strength of your faith because it doesn't always feel perfect or unwavering? How might embracing the idea that faith is a journey, not a destination, help you view your imperfections as part of growing closer to God?

_____
_____
_____
_____
_____
_____
_____
_____
_____
_____

Reflect on a moment when your vulnerability or honesty about your faith encouraged someone else. How did that impact you both?

_____
_____
_____
_____
_____
_____
_____
_____
_____
_____

What did you learn from this chapter about how perspective shapes our experiences? In your own life, what are you focusing on—are you amplifying your challenges, or are you shifting your attention to the blessings and opportunities before you?

___

Think about the places you frequent—your workplace, neighborhood, or social groups. How are you using those spaces to reflect God's love?

___

Reflect on a seemingly insignificant action or conversation that later had a profound impact. How does that experience challenge you to be more intentional in your daily interactions?

_____
_____
_____
_____
_____
_____
_____
_____
_____

CHAPTER 16

HAPPY MOTHER'S DAY, JEAN!

*Faith isn't just about receiving;
it's about enduring.*

READING TIME

As you read Chapter 16: "Happy Mother's Day, Jean!" in *Two and a Half Acres of Faith*, review, reflect on, and respond to the text by answering the following questions.

REVIEW, REFLECT, AND RESPOND

How long have you been waiting for your promise or dream to come to pass? What is your current level of faith in believing that God will bring His promise to fulfillment?

_____
_____
_____
_____
_____
_____
_____
_____
_____

What's the longest you've ever had to wait for a miracle? What did you do in the waiting? How did you handle doubt and discouragement?

_____
_____
_____
_____
_____
_____
_____
_____
_____

What big things do you think God can do with your endurance and perseverance right now as you wait for your miracle? In what ways could the waiting be God's way of protecting you, rather than withholding a good gift from you?

_____
_____
_____
_____
_____
_____
_____

Reflect on the joy you experienced when a long-awaited prayer was finally answered. What made the waiting worthwhile?

_____
_____
_____
_____
_____
_____
_____
_____

What have you learned about the power of prayer? What have you wrestled with, and what questions are you waiting for to be answered?

_____
_____
_____

Reflect on the spiritual legacy you have received, whether positive or negative. How has it influenced your faith journey, and what direction are you currently taking in building the legacy you hope to leave behind?

What three key lessons from this book will you carry forward and apply as you dedicate your heart, efforts, and every aspect of your life to serving God?

CHAPTER 17

WE BUILT A FAMILY

> *Your two-and-a-half acres of faith may look different from mine, but it will be just as meaningful, just as miraculous, and just as life-changing.*

READING TIME

As you read Chapter 17: "We Built a Family" in *Two and a Half Acres of Faith*, review, reflect on, and respond to the text by answering the following questions.

REVIEW, REFLECT, AND RESPOND

What important relationship in your life have you had to build on grace and forgiveness? What kind of challenges have you faced, and what have you learned?

_____
_____
_____
_____
_____
_____
_____
_____

What small memories from your past stand out as profoundly joyful or impactful? What makes them so meaningful, and how do they fit into the greater story God is weaving in your life and family?

_____
_____
_____
_____
_____
_____
_____
_____

What insights did this chapter give you about trusting that seeds of faith are being planted, even when they don't seem visible or apparent?

Why is remaining faithful during difficult times so essential? What has this book taught you about the lasting impact that unwavering faithfulness to God can create?

What does your own "two-and-a-half acres of faith" journey look like? Where do you find yourself in that journey now, and where do you sense God is leading you next?

_____
_____
_____
_____
_____
_____
_____
_____
_____

What three key lessons from this book will you carry forward and apply as you dedicate your heart, efforts, and every aspect of your life to serving God?

_____
_____
_____
_____
_____
_____
_____
_____
_____
_____
_____
_____